'MY HEART BRIMS WITH BILLOWS AND MINNOWS OF SHADOWS AND SILVER.'

FEDERICO GARCÍA LORCA
Born 1898, Fuente Vaqueros, Granada, Spain
Died 1936, between Víznar and Alfacar, Granada, Spain

A representative sampling of Federico García Lorca's poetry,
dialogues, and short prose. Included here are very well known
and some lesser-known works, some of which appear in
English for the first time, ranging from Lorca's earliest poetry
to his renowned *Gypsy Ballads* and posthumous publications.

GARCÍA LORCA IN PENGUIN MODERN CLASSICS
The House of Bernarda Alba and Other Plays
Poet in New York
Selected Poems

FEDERICO GARCÍA LORCA

The Dialogue of Two Snails

Translated from the Spanish by Tyler Fisher

PENGUIN BOOKS

PENGUIN CLASSICS

UK | USA | Canada | Ireland | Australia
India | New Zealand | South Africa

Penguin Books is part of the Penguin Random House group
of companies whose addresses can be found at
global.penguinrandomhouse.com.

This selection first published 2018
003

Set in 9.85 / 12.75 pt Dante MT Std
Typeset by Jouve (UK), Milton Keynes
Printed and bound in Great Britain by Clays Ltd, Elcograf S.p.A.

ISBN: 978-0-241-34040-0

www.greenpenguin.co.uk

MIX
Paper from
responsible sources
FSC® C018179

Contents

The Dialogue of Two Snails

White Snail.– *(Silence.)*
(A young lady with a lace parasol comes along counting her steps. Upon reaching a little brook, she hesitates. Then she jumps.)

Black Snail.– *(Silence.)*
(The rat has crossed the river. The bad rat. The rat that devours the tender rootlets.)

White Snail.– *(Silence.)*
(The young lady consults the scent of the fennel beds. The evening, lacking intelligent relations, crumbles down into the haze of the horizon.)

Black Snail.– *(Silence.)*
(The rat returns to the blackberry bushes. An obscure voice delights in pronouncing this word: blackberry, blackberry, blackberry.)

White Snail.– *(Pause.)*
(The young lady sits down on the green hillside. She has come outside alone because she does not recall the mice.)

Black Snail.–(*Dumbstruck.*)   (*Silence.*)
(*In the watery cove, with nary a crease, a long cloud quivers in place. The rat heads for it like a bird. The Lord must have consented to his inflicting this abuse.*)

White Snail.–   (*Silence.*)
(*No one likes the book the young lady is reading. She is silly, unaware that her mountains of sugar are full of ants.*)

Black Snail.–   (*Exit.*)

White Snail.–(*At the top of the fennel stalk.*)
Ay!

(February 1926)

The Encounters of an Adventurous Snail

December 1918
(Granada)

to Ramón P. Roda

There is a childlike sweetness
in the still morning.
The trees stretch
their arms to the earth.
A tremulous vapour
blankets the seed-beds,
and the spiders unfurl
their silken roads
– rigging streaks upon the pure crystal
of the air.

    In the poplar grove
a burbling spring recites
its song among the sedges.
And the snail, the peaceful
bourgeois of the narrow trail,
contemplates the landscape.
The divine serenity
of Nature

gave him courage and faith,
and, forgetting the troubles
of his home, he longed
to see the end of the path.

He set off, and slipped into
a forest of ivy
and nettles. In its midst
were two old frogs
basking in the sun,
listless and sickly.

'Those modern songs,'
one of them muttered,
'are useless.' 'Absolutely,
my friend,' replied
the other frog, who was
maimed and almost blind,
'When I was young I believed
that, in the end, if God heard
our singing, He would have
mercy. But the knowledge
I have gained in my long life
makes me disbelieve it.
I no longer sing . . .'

The two frogs grumble,
begging alms
from a new frogling,

who smugly passes by,
pushing aside the sedges in her path.

Facing the gloomy forest
the snail pauses in terror.
He wants to scream. He cannot.
The frogs approach him.

'Is it a butterfly?'
says the frog that is almost blind.
'It has two little horns,'
the other frog answers,
'It is the snail. Have you come,
Snail, from other lands?'

'I've come from my house, and I'd like
to return home very soon.'
'A very cowardly critter,'
exclaims the blind frog.
'Do you ever sing?' 'I do not sing,'
says the snail. 'And don't you pray?'
'No, I never learned.'
'Don't you believe in eternal life?'
'What is that?'
'It's living forever
in the most placid water
alongside a richly flowering land
abounding in delicacies.'

'One day, when I was very young,
my poor old grandmother told me
that when I die I would rise
upon the softest leaves
of the highest trees.'

'Your grandmother was a heretic.
We are telling you the truth,
You shall believe in it,'
say the frogs enraged.

'Why ever did I long to see the path?'
groans the snail. 'Yes, I do believe,
ever and always, in the eternal life
you preach to me . . .'
The frogs,
deep in thought, withdraw,
and the snail, dismayed,
slips away into the thicket.

The two maundering frogs
sit there like sphinxes.
One of them asks:
'Do you believe in eternal life?'
'Not I,' the blind, maimed frog
replies with great sadness.
'Then why did we tell
the snail to believe?'
'Because . . . I don't know why,'

says the blind frog.
'I swell with emotion
on hearing the conviction
with which my children call out
to God from the ditch . . .'

The poor snail turns back
the way he came. Along the path
an undulating silence now
flows from the poplar grove.
He now encounters a group
of ants the colour of flesh.
They are almost rioting,
dragging behind them
another ant whose antennae
are badly mangled.
The snail exclaims:
'Little Ants, forbear!
Why are you mistreating
your companion in this way?
Tell me what she has done.
I will judge in good conscience.
Tell me yourself, little Ant.'

The ant, half-dead,
says very sadly:
'I have seen the stars.'
'What are stars?' say
the little ants uneasily.

And the snail, deep in thought,
asks, 'Stars?'
'Yes,' the ant repeats,
'I have seen the stars;
I climbed the highest tree
in the poplar grove,
and saw thousands of eyes
in my own darkness.'
The snail asks,
'But what are the stars?'
'They are lights we carry
above our heads.'
'We do not see them,'
the ants remark.
And the snail adds: 'My eyesight
reaches only as high as the grass.'

Waggling their antennae,
the ants clamour:
'We shall kill you, for you are
a lazy and perverse ant.
Work is your law.'

'I have seen the stars,'
says the injured ant.
And the snail declares:
'Let her go,
and carry on with your toils.
Shattered and spent,
she will likely die very soon.'

Through the sickeningly-sweet air,
a bee drifts by.
The ant, in the throes of death,
inhales the vast eventide,
and says, 'It is she who comes
to carry me off to a star.'

The other little ants
flee when they see she has died.

The snail sighs
and departs, bewildered,
full of confusion
regarding the eternal. 'The path
has no end,' he exclaims.
'Perhaps one could reach
the stars from here.
But my lowly dullness
will hinder my arrival.'

All was hazy
in the feeble sunlight and fog.
Distant belfries
summon people to church,
and the snail, the peaceful
bourgeois of the narrow trail,
bewildered and uneasy,
contemplates the landscape.

Tree of Surprises

SOCRATES

The philosopher arrived at the circle of his disciples. In the centre – its bulb closed and freshly bedewed by the young eyes – loomed a great onion of ideas. Everyone sharpened their tongues and made ready to peel away its layered skin. An evening moon melted away among the foliage.

The onion began to spin; its layers of skin, the colour of gold, the colour of amethyst, glittered at the moment of being torn away. Socrates smiled enigmatically; his disciples smiled, swathed in the crimson of their faith: the onion filled with golden and black stars like an altar-piece sky, and all said: 'There it is!' . . . Then the ideal vegetable dwindled away until it disappeared in delicate, imperceptible gauzes . . . and everyone left.

Far away, Lysis danced on a pyramid of stagnant wind.

II

The philosopher withdrew from the circle of his disciples. The evening folded its silken tent, and the whole sky seemed to be covered by a translucent onion skin. Socrates saw a firefly. Socrates heard a toad. Socrates saw an enormous butterfly towards the South . . . and a little red snake lit up the philosopher's entire chest, like a bleeding gash from an axe, like a wound reflected. Then he vanished into the confluence of winds.

In the Garden of Lunar Grapefruit

Like a shadow our life slips away, never to return;
nor shall aught of us or ours return.

Pero López de Ayala, *Moral Advice*

I have said goodbye to the friends I love most, so as to embark upon a brief but dramatic voyage. On a silver mirror, long before the break of day, I find the valise of clothes I must wear in the strange land to which I am heading.

The tense, cold fragrance of daybreak mysteriously batters the vast, sheer cliff of the night.

On the glossy page of the sky, the first letter of a cloud was trembling, and beneath my balcony a nightingale and a frog raise aloft a sleepy criss-cross of sound.

Calm yet melancholic, I make my final preparations, hindered by the subtlest emotions of wings and concentric circles. On the white wall of my room hangs the glorious sword, stiff and rigid like a serpent in a museum – the sword my grandfather carried in the war against Don Carlos de Borbón.

With reverence, I take down that sword coated in yellowish rust like a white poplar, and gird it on, recalling that I will have to undergo a great invisible battle before entering the garden. An ecstatic and brutal battle with my age-old enemy, the gigantic dragon of Common Sense.

A sharp emotion, like an elegy for the things that have never been – good things and bad, large things and small – invades the landscapes of my eyes, which are almost hidden behind a pair of violet-tinted glasses. A bitter emotion that compels me to walk towards this quivering garden on the highest prairies of the air.

The eyes of every creature patter like phosphorescent dots against the wall of the future . . . what is past remains filled with yellow undergrowth, orchards without fruit and rivers without water. No man ever toppled backwards onto death. But, when momentarily contemplating that desolate, infinite landscape, I have seen drafts of unpublished life – multiple, overlapping drafts, like the buckets on an endless water-wheel.

Before setting off, I feel a sharp pain in my heart. My family is asleep, and the entire house is steeped in utter repose. The dawn, unveiling towers and counting, one by one, the leaves of the trees, robes me in crackling, luminescent lace.

I am forgetting something . . . there's not the slightest doubt in my mind . . . so much time spent getting ready! and . . . Lord, what am I forgetting? Aha! A block of wood . . . a good, dense block of blushing cherry wood. I believe that one should step out looking dapper . . . From a vase of flowers on my nightstand, I fasten in my left buttonhole a large, pale rose, which has an enraged but inscrutable, priestly face.

Now the time has come.

(On the jagged platters of the clanging bells, come the roosters' cock-a-doodle-doos.)

Telegraph

The station was desolate. One man was going and another was coming. At times the tongue of the bell wet its round lips with stuttering sounds. From within, one could hear the telegraph's intermittent rosary. I lay down with my face to the sky and, without thinking, went off to a strange country where I encountered no one, a country that floated on a blue-bleak river. Little by little I noticed that the air was filling with yellowish bubbles, which my breath melted away. It was the telegraph. Its *tick-tock* entered the vast antennae of my ears with the rhythm of muscid mosquitos over a pond. The station was desolate. I looked indolently at the sky and saw that all the stars were sending telegraphs with their luminous twinkling. Sirius, above them all, sent out orange *ticks* and green *tocks* amid the astonishment of all the others.

The luminous telegraph of the sky merged with the poor telegraph of the station, and my soul (far too tender) answered with its eyelids all the questions and flirtations of the stars, which I then understood perfectly.

Scene of the Lieutenant Colonel of the Civil Guard

(Flag-festooned guardroom)

LIEUTENANT COLONEL
I am the Lieutenant Colonel of the Civil Guard.

SERGEANT
Yes, sir.

LIEUTENANT COLONEL
And no one contradicts me.

SERGEANT
No, sir.

LIEUTENANT COLONEL
I've got three stars and twenty crosses.

SERGEANT
Yes, sir.

LIEUTENANT COLONEL
The Cardinal Archbishop has hailed me with his twenty-four purple tassels.

SERGEANT
Yes, sir.

LIEUTENANT COLONEL

I am the lieutenant. I am the lieutenant. I am the
lieutenant colonel of the Civil Guard.
(*Romeo and Juliet – sky-blue, white, and gold – embrace over
the tobacco garden on the box of cigars. The soldier caresses the
barrel of a rifle filled with undersea shadows. A voice from
outside.*)

Moon, moon, moon, moon,
olive season's coming soon.
Cazorla Town displays her tower,
and Benamejí conceals it.

Moon, moon, moon, moon.
A cockerel crows on the moon.
O Mayor, beware: your little girls
are gazing at the moon.

LIEUTENANT COLONEL

What's going on?

SERGEANT

A gypsy!
(*The little gypsy's gaze, like that of a young mule, darkens and
bloats the baggy blinkers of the* Lieutenant Colonel *of the
Civil Guard.*)

LIEUTENANT COLONEL

I am the lieutenant colonel of the Civil Guard.

GYPSY
Yes.

LIEUTENANT COLONEL
Who are you?

GYPSY
A gypsy.

LIEUTENANT COLONEL
And what, pray tell, is a gypsy?

GYPSY
Anything whatever.

LIEUTENANT COLONEL
What is your name?

GYPSY
Just that.

LIEUTENANT COLONEL
That what, you say?

GYPSY
Gypsy.

SERGEANT
I found him and brought him in.

LIEUTENANT COLONEL
Where were you?

GYPSY
On the bridge over the rivers.

LIEUTENANT COLONEL
But, over what rivers?

GYPSY
Over all rivers.

LIEUTENANT COLONEL
And what were you doing there?

GYPSY
Making a cinnamon tower.

LIEUTENANT COLONEL
Sergeant!

SERGEANT
At your command, my lieutenant colonel of the Civil Guard.

GYPSY
I have invented wings to fly, and I do fly. Brimstone and roses on my lips.

LIEUTENANT COLONEL
Ay!

GYPSY
But I don't need wings, for I can fly without them. Clouds and rings in my blood.

LIEUTENANT COLONEL
Ayy!

GYPSY
In January, I have orange blossoms.

LIEUTENANT COLONEL (*writhing*)
Ayyyyy!

GYPSY
And oranges in the snow.

LIEUTENANT COLONEL
Ayyyyy! wham, whomp, whump. (*He falls down dead*)
(*The soul of the Lieutenant Colonel of the Civil Guard, a mingling of tobacco and coffee with frothy milk, exits through the window.*)

SERGEANT
Help!
(*In the barracks yard, four civil guards flog the little gypsy.*)

Song of the Battered Gypsy

Twenty-four resounding blows.
Twenty-five resounding blows.
Then, by night, my mother goes,
lays me out on silver foil.

Civil Guards who range the roads,
grant me but some sips of water.
Water filled with fish and boats.
Water, water, water, water.

Guv'nor of the Civil Guard,
yonder in your lofty hall!
Surely you've no scraps of lace,
ay, for me to wipe my face!

5 July 1925

Riddle of the Guitar

In the round
crossroads,
six maidens
dance.
Three of flesh
and three of silver.
Dreams of yesterday pursue them from afar,
but a golden Polyphemus
clasps them in his arms.
The guitar!

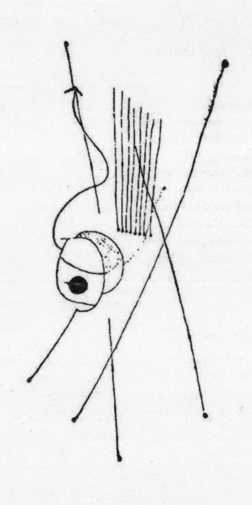

The Six Strings

The guitar
draws tears from dreams.
The sobbing of lost
souls
seeps from its round
mouth.
And like the tarantula
it weaves a vast star
to catch sighs,
which float in its dark
wooden reservoir.

Castanet

Castanet.
Castanet.
Castanet.
Beetle rattle resonant.

In the supple spider
of the hand
you curl the sultry
air,
and plunge into your timbered
trill.

Castanet.
Castanet.
Castanet.

Conjuring

The convulsing hand
like a medusa
blinds the doleful eye
of the oil-lamp.

Ace of clubs.
Sign of the scissory cross.

Above the white smoke
of incense, it has
something akin to a burrowing mole and
indecisive butterfly.

Ace of clubs.
Sign of the scissory cross.

It clutches an invisible
heart. Do you see the hand clutching?
A heart
reflected in the wind.

Ace of clubs.
Sign of the scissory cross.

Knell

In yellow
towers
toll the bells.

On yellow
winds,
unfold the tolling.

Crowned with withered
orange blossoms, Death
goes down a road.
She sings and sings
a song
upon her white guitar of yore,
and sings and sings and sings.

In yellow towers
halt the bells.

The wind and dust
make silver prows.

Song

Knock knock.
Who's there?
The Autumn once again.
What does the Autumn want?
The summer freshness of your head.
I do not want to yield it to you.
Yet I want to wrest it from you.

Knock knock.
Who's there?
The Autumn once again.

(Madrid, 1933)

Quasi-Elegy

So much living.
All for what?
The path is flat and dreary,
and there is not love enough.

So much hurry.
All for what?
To board the boat
that has no port.
My friends, return!
Return to your wellspring!
Pour not out your soul
into the vessel
of Death.

Landscape

The plain
of olive trees
unfolds and closes
like a fan.
Above the rows of olive trees,
a sunken sky
and murky rain
of cold day-stars.
Reed and half-lit shadow quiver
at the edges of the river.
The grey air ripples into pleats.
The olive trees
display their freight
of shrieks.
A skein
of birds encaged,
that sway their long, long
tail-plumes in the haze.

Trees

1919

Trees!
Were you once feathered darts
that hurtled from the blue?
What fearsome warriors fired you?
Was it the stars?

Your music flows from souls of birds,
from God's own eyes,
from perfect passion.
Trees!
Will your rugged root-tips recognize
my heart amid the earth?

Field

1920

The sky is ash.
The trees are white,
and burnt coal-black
the stubble stripes.
The Sunset's wound
is bleeding dry,
and ridges crease
bleak paper heights.
The roadside dust
in gullies hides.
The springs raise silt;
the coves subside.
In reddish grey
the sheep-shear chimes,
and motherlike, the waterwheel
has rounded off its rosary.

The sky is ash.
The trees are white.

They Felled Three Trees

to Ernesto Halffter

They were three.
(Day brought its axes to bear.)
They were two.
(Silver wings raking the air.)
There was one.
There were none.
(The water was stripped bleak and bare.)

Street of the Wordless Ones

Behind the stone-still windowpanes,
the girls play with their laughter.

(In the empty pianos,
acrobatic spider puppeteers.)

The girls speak with their lovers,
fluttering their tight braids.

(World of the folding fan,
handkerchief, and hand.)

The suitors answer back, fashioning
wings and flowers with their sable capes.

Tree of Song

for Ana María Dalí

Reed of gesture, voice, and face,
time and time again
quakes and quavers, void of hope,
in the air of yesterday.

Long the girl had sighed,
long she ached to grasp it – yet
always reached the place
one minute too late.

Ay, Sun! *Ay*, moon, moon!,
one minute too late.
Sixty flowers, wan and grey,
tangled round her feet.

Look at how she swings and sways
time and time again,
maiden made of bough and bloom,
in the air of yesterday.

Seashell

to Natalita Jiménez

They've brought me a seashell.

Its depths sing an atlas
of seascapes downriver.
My heart
brims with billows
and minnows
of shadows and silver.

They've brought me a seashell.

Cradle Song

to Mercedes, after death

Now we see you fast asleep.
Your driftwood boat is rocking by the shore.

Pale princess of nevermore.
Slumber through the darkest night!
Snowy body, snowy earth.
Sleep through sunrise, sleep through light!

Now you slip away in sleep.
Your boat is sea-mist, dreaming, by the shore.

Gypsy Zorongo

In needlework, my lovelorn hands
are crafting you a cape,
its edges trimmed with gillyblooms,
its cowl of water made.

When you were still a man of mine,
amid the white springtide,
the echo of your horse's hooves
four heaving, silver sighs.

The moon is just a shallow well,
the flowers all for naught.
Your arms alone hold value now
when holding me at night.
Your arms alone hold value now
when holding me at night.

Federico García Lorca.
Oma A.e 1937

The Moon and Death

1919

The moon has teeth of ivory.
How old and sad she looms!
The riverbeds are dry,
the fields devoid of green;
the trees, so wan and sere,
are stripped of leaves and nests.
And wrinkled Lady Death
now walks the willow groves,
her court absurdly formed
of empty, far-fetched hopes.
She's hawking hues of wax
and shades of thunderstorms, –
a fairy from a tale:
a wicked busybones.

The moon has purchased paints
from Death's prismatic greys.
Tonight, a turbid night,
the moon is raving mad!

For my part, I have launched
a tuneless festival:
its site, my sombre heart;
its tents, the shadow's gloom.

Ballad of the Moon, Moon

to Conchita García Lorca

The moon arose: her stage the forge,
her bustle spiced with lavender.
The child watches, watches her;
his eyes are watching her.
A rousing dance bestirs the air:
the moon contorts her limbs
and flaunts – lubricious, sleek, and pure –
her breasts of solid tin.

–Be on your way now, moon, moon, moon.
If gypsies come, take heed:
they'd take apart your heart to make
white rings and strings of beads.
–Boy, leave me be, and let me dance.
When gypsies come tonight,
they'll find you on the anvil block,
your little eyes closed tight.
–I hear the gypsies' horses now.
Be on your way, moon, moon,
–Boy, leave me be. Don't tread upon
my starched white clair-de-lune.

The horseman thrummed the flatland drum,
its cadence drawing nigh,
and, lo, inside the silent forge,
the child closed his eyes.

In bronze, in dreams, the gypsies came
across the olive grove,
their heads held high against the sky,
their hooded eyes half-closed.

The nightbird on her tree-bough sings,
as only nightbirds can!
Across the sky, the moon drifts by,
a child by the hand.

The gypsies weep within the forge;
they weep with shouts and sobs.
The wind above keeps watch and ward.
The wind is keeping watch.

The Gypsy Nun

to José Moreno Villa

Silence thick with lime and myrtle.
Mallows in the windlestraw.
The nun embroiders gillyflowers
on a field of flaxen cloth.
From the grizzled spider lantern
seven prism-birds erupt.
Far away the church is grumbling,
like a bear turned belly-up.
Splendid needlework! How graceful!
On her flaxen tapestry,
she is yearning to embroider
flowers of her fantasy.
Daisies and magnolias glisten:
ribbon tendrils, spangled gauze!
Saffron crocuses and moonbeams,
stitched upon the altar cloth!
Five red grapefruits slowly sweeten
on the nearby kitchen sill.
Christ's five wounds, nasturtium blossoms,
cut in Almería's hills.
Then two highwaymen come riding,
galloping across her eyes.

One last muffled tremor rumbles,
strips away the nun's attire.
As she gazes at the clouds and
hills in rigid faraways,
her heart of lemon-tinged verbena,
citrus mixed with sugar, breaks.
Oh, what flatlands, sheer and soaring,
lit by twenty suns on high!
Oh, what rivers rearing upward,
as her fantasy descries!
But she keeps on with her flowers,
while the rampant light still plays
chess aloft, in chequered breezes,
through the latticed window grate.

Tamar and Amnon

for Alfonso García Valdecasas

The moon wheels round the sky
above the thirsty plains,
while summer scatters rumbling seeds
of tiger purrs and flame.
Far overhead, the roofs rang out
with metal nerves that shriek.
A curly wind came rippling in
with tufts of woolly bleats.
The earth displays its skin arrayed
in lesions laced with scars,
or jolted by the piercing white
of cauterizing sparks.

*

Tamar was dreaming dreams of birds
that nestled in her throat,
with sounds of chilly tambourines
and zithers' moon-strung notes.
Her artful nude upon the eaves,
acute north palm aligned,
pleads snowflakes of her abdomen
and hailstones of her spine.

Tamar was singing in the nude;
the terraced roof her realm,
while all around her unshod feet
five frozen doves lie numb.
Amnon, so sleek and concrete, watched
her from the tower's brow.
His loins were lathered full of foam,
his beard aquiver, up and down.
Her lustrous nude lay stretched upon
the terrace, with a throb
half mumbled through one's teeth, as of
an arrow freshly lodged.
Amnon beheld the bulbous moon
drift low towards the west,
and in the buxom moon he saw
his sister's solid breasts.

*

Amnon, at half-past three o'clock,
across his bed reclined.
All corners of that chamber ached
with wings that filled his eyes.
The light, congealed and thick, entombs
whole towns in dusky sand,
or brings out roses, dahlias,
in fleeting coral strands.
The sap of wellsprings long suppressed
sprouts silence in the urns.
Amid the tree trunks' mats of moss

the sprawling cobra croons.
Amnon now moans among the cold,
crisp linens of his bed.
An ivy shiver of the chills
conceals his broiled flesh.
Tamar in silence entered in
the silent, silenced room,
imbued with veins and Danube streams,
disturbed by distant residues.
–Tamar, erase my eyes
with your unmoving dawn.
My threads of blood will intertwine
as frills along your hem.
–My brother, leave me be in peace.
Your kisses on my spine
are wasps and spindly winds that form
twin swarms of reedy pipes.
–Tamar, your lofty bosom holds
two fish that bid me come,
and in your tender fingertips
a sheltered rosebud hums.

*

The hundred horses of the king
were neighing in the yard.
Against the vats of sun, the vines
of slenderness strained hard.
By turns he grabs her by the hair,
then rakes her shift in shreds.

The streams of tepid corals streak
a map of muted red.

*

Oh, what a host of cries were heard
above the houses, oh!
What bristling density of blades
and lacerated robes.
Along the dismal stairs the slaves
are climbing up and down,
while thighs and pistons play as one
beneath the standing clouds.
Around Tamar the gypsies throng:
the gypsy virgins wail,
and others gather up the drops
her martyred flower spills.
In chambers locked and shuttered now
white linens seem to blush
The muttered hums of tepid dawn
change tendril sprigs and fish.

*

Amnon, a ravisher enraged,
takes flight astride his nag.
From battlements and barbicans
black archers mark his back.
And when the fourfold hooves became
four fading echo-hooves,
then David drew his shears and cut
his harp strings through and through.

Each Song

Each song
is a tide pool
of love.

Each day-star
a tide pool
of time.
A knot
of time.

And each sigh
a tide pool
of a cry.

Notes

Dialogue of the Two Snails ('Diálogo de los dos caracoles'): published posthumously in *Tres diálogos*, ed. Manuel Fernández-Montesinos (Granada, 1985).

The Encounters of an Adventurous Snail ('Los encuentros de un caracol aventurero'): from *Libro de poemas* (Madrid, 1921). The ellipses are Lorca's own.

Tree of Surprises ('Árbol de sorpresas'): published posthumously in *Federico García Lorca, heterodoxo y mártir*, ed. Eutimio Martín (Madrid, 1986).

In the Garden of Lunar Grapefruit ('En el jardín de las toronjas de luna'): published posthumously. The ellipses are Lorca's own.
Don Carlos de Borbón: Lorca chooses a deliberately ambiguous title, which can apply to various monarchs, princes, and pretenders to the throne in the Bourbon dynasty.

Telegraph ('Telégrafo'): published posthumously.

Scene of the Lieutenant Colonel of the Civil Guard ('Escena del Teniente Coronel de la Guardia Civil'): from *Poema del cante jondo* (Madrid, 1931).

Riddle of the Guitar ('Adivinanza de la guitarra'): from *Poema del cante jondo* (Madrid, 1931).

The Six Strings ('Las seis cuerdas'): from *Poema del cante jondo* (Madrid, 1931).

Castanet ('Crótalo'): from *Poema del cante jondo* (Madrid, 1931).

Conjuring ('Conjuro'): from *Poema del cante jondo* (Madrid, 1931).

Sign of the scissory cross: Placing open scissors, in the form of a cross, on the roof of a house or under one's bed, is a Southern Spanish folk superstition meant to ward off devils or witches.

Knell ('Clamor'): from *Poema del cante jondo* (Madrid, 1931).

Song ('Canción'): a poem Lorca included in his lecture, 'Cómo canta una ciudad de noviembre a noviembre' (October 1933).

Quasi-Elegy ('Casi-Elegía'): published as part of 'Suite del regreso' in *La Verdad* 2.18 (Málaga, May 1924).

Landscape ('Paisaje'): from *Poema del cante jondo* (Madrid, 1931).

Trees ('Árboles'): from *Libro de poemas* (Madrid, 1921).

Field ('Campo'): from *Libro de poemas* (Madrid, 1921).

They Felled Three Trees ('Cortaron tres árboles'): from *Canciones* (Málaga, 1927).

Street of the Wordless Ones ('La calle de los mudos'): from *Canciones* (Málaga, 1927).

Tree of Song ('Árbol de canción'): from *Canciones* (Málaga, 1927). Lorca dedicated the poem to Salvador Dalí's younger sister, with whom he maintained a long friendship and correspondence.

Seashell ('Caracola'): from *Canciones* (Málaga, 1927).

Cradle Song ('Canción de cuna'): Lorca wrote this lullaby for Mercedes Yebes, who died while still a child in May 1936, three months before the poet's own assassination.

Gypsy Zorongo ('Zorongo gitano'): *Zorongo* is a traditional form of flamenco song and dance.

The Moon and Death ('La luna y la muerte'): from *Libro de poemas* (Madrid, 1921).

Ballad of the Moon, Moon ('Romance de la luna, luna'): from *Romancero gitano* (Madrid, 1928). Lorca dedicated this poem to his younger sister, María de la Concepción 'Conchita' García Lorca.

The Gypsy Nun ('La monja gitana'): from *Romancero gitano*. The poem is dedicated to José Moreno Villa, a poet, painter, and editor with whom Lorca developed a friendship at the Residencia de Estudiantes, Madrid.

Tamar and Amnon ('Thamar y Amnón'): from *Romancero gitano*. Lorca dedicated the poem to Alfonso García Valdecasas, a university classmate in Granada.

Each Song ('Cada canción'): Untitled in Lorca's manuscript, this poem is conventionally designated by its first line.